D1431435

TEXTUAL
CRITICISM

TEXTUAL CRITICISM

BY

PAUL MAAS

TRANSLATED FROM THE GERMAN BY

BARBARA FLOWER

OXFORD
AT THE CLARENDON PRESS

Oxford University Press, Ely House, London W. 1

GLASGOW   NEW YORK   TORONTO   MELBOURNE   WELLINGTON
CAPE TOWN   SALISBURY   IBADAN   NAIROBI   LUSAKA   ADDIS ABABA
BOMBAY   CALCUTTA   MADRAS   KARACHI   LAHORE   DACCA
KUALA LUMPUR   HONG KONG   TOKYO

Originally published in German under the title *Textkritik* in 1927 as Part VII of Gercke–Norden, *Einleitung in die Altertumswissenschaft*, Vol. I, 3rd ed. A second edition was published separately by the firm of B. G. Teubner of Leipzig in 1949, and a third edition in 1957.

PUBLISHED 1958
REPRINTED LITHOGRAPHICALLY AT THE
UNIVERSITY PRESS, OXFORD
1963, 1967

PREFACE

This translation was originally made from the second (1949) German edition, but in preparing it for the Press occasion has been taken to include the changes incorporated in the third (1957) German edition, including the *Retrospect 1956*.

To Miss Barbara Flower, to her father, the late Dr. Robin Flower, and to his whole family I owe much more than I can say here. She died, aged 43, in 1955, before I had the opportunity of discussing with her the manuscript of her translation. For translating the *Retrospect 1956* my thanks go to Mr. C. H. Roberts, Secretary to the Delegates of the University Press. During the proof-reading most effective help was given by Mr. H. Lloyd-Jones.

P. M.

Oxford, March 1958

PREFACE

PREFACE TO THE
SECOND (GERMAN) EDITION

THE first edition of this essay (published in 1927) was reviewed with great kindness and in great detail by G. Pasquali in 1929 (in *Gnomon*, v. 417 ff.). Pasquali's own investigations made in connexion with my essay (in *Gnomon*, v. 498 ff. and in his *Storia della tradizione e critica del testo*, 1934) deal in the main with topics closely related to but excluded from my presentation, i.e. with the history of transmission of the individual texts and 'contaminated' traditions, which of course cannot be systematically disentangled. I myself published in 1937 a brief statement of the principles of 'stemmatics' ('Leitfehler und stemmatische Typen', *Byz. Zeitschr.* xxxvii. 289 ff.) and collaborated from 1936 to 1938 in the preparation of W. Quandt's critical edition of the Orphic Hymns (1941). I contributed a short account of the subject to the *Oxford Classical Dictionary* (1949), s.v. Textual Criticism, where I referred also to related problems in the text of Shakespeare.

In the present edition the text of the first is repeated with several changes. Some additions are indicated by the sign [1949]. The above-mentioned essay on 'indicative errors', a topic which has received very little attention, has been added as an appendix. Its subject-matter is much the same as that of the chapter on *recensio*, but the mode of approach is so different that it seemed best not to work the two accounts into one.

Oxford, 19 July 1949

CONTENTS

A. BASIC NOTIONS

1. We have no autograph manuscripts of the Greek and Roman classical writers and no copies which have been collated with the originals; the manuscripts we possess derive from the originals through an unknown number of intermediate copies, and are consequently of questionable trustworthiness.

The business of textual criticism is to produce a text as close as possible to the original (*constitutio textus*).

A dictation revised by the author must be regarded as equivalent to an autograph manuscript.

2. In each individual case the original text either has or has not been transmitted. So our first task is to establish what *must* or *may* be regarded as transmitted—to make the recension (*recensio*); our next is to examine this tradition and discover whether it may be considered as giving the original (*examinatio*); if it proves not to give the original, we must try to reconstruct the original by conjecture (*divinatio*) or at least to isolate the corruption.

In the usual division of textual criticism into *recensio* and *emendatio* two cases are left out of account—that where examination leads to the conclusion that the text is *either* sound *or* irremediable, and that where the original can only be established by choosing (*selectio*) between different traditions of equal 'stemmatical'[1] value.

[1] Cf. Appendix I.

B. RECENSIO

(cf. § 25)

3. The tradition rests either on a single witness (*codex unicus*) or on several.

In the former case *recensio* consists in describing and deciphering as accurately as possible the single witness; in the latter it is often a very complicated business.

4. Each witness depends either on a surviving or on a lost *exemplar*. If it depends on a lost exemplar, this lost exemplar either can or cannot be reconstructed. If it can be reconstructed, this may be done either without the aid of the witness or only with its help.

It will now be obvious that a witness is worthless (worthless, that is, *qua* witness) when it depends exclusively on a surviving exemplar or on an exemplar which can be reconstructed without its help. A witness thus shown to be worthless (cf. § 8) must be *eliminated* (*eliminatio codicum descriptorum*).

5. If there still remain several witnesses after the *eliminandi* have been excluded (§ 4), then we have a *split* in the tradition. This can only arise if two or more copies were made from a single exemplar; the 'branches' of the tradition arising in this way appear in the surviving witnesses, with or without further splits (*intermediate* splits).

The exemplar from which the first split originated we call the *archetype*. The text of this archetype is free from all errors arising after the split and is therefore closer to the original than the text of any of the witnesses. If we succeed then in establishing the text of this, the *constitutio* (recon-struction of the original) is considerably advanced.

The special importance of the exemplar which I have termed the archetype is not contested, and there is no other name available. For this reason we should be careful not to use the term archetype of other connecting links between the original and the surviving witnesses, however important they may be at times. [This reminder has again become very necessary at the present time. 1956.]

6. In what follows it is assumed (1) that the copies made since the primary split in the tradition each reproduce one exemplar only, i.e. that no scribe has combined several exemplars (*contaminatio*), (2) that each scribe consciously or unconsciously deviates from his exemplar, i.e. makes '*peculiar errors*'.

On the consequences of a different set of assumptions see §§ 9, 10, 11.

7. On these assumptions it becomes possible in general (*a*) to demonstrate incontestably the interrelationship of all surviving witnesses, as well as the number and position of all intermediate splits in the tradition, (*b*) where the primary split is into at least *three* branches, to reconstruct with cer-tainty the text of the archetype at all places (with a few exceptions to be accounted for separately), (*c*) if the primary split is into *two* branches, to restore the text of the archetype to a point where (again with exceptions to be separately accounted for) we have at no place more than two readings (*variants*) from which to choose.

8. A typical instance (see Diagram). Given are the wit-nesses A to J (not K), all differing in date and in kind (manu-scripts, printed copies, epitomes, excerpts, paraphrases, quotations, imitations, translations, &c.). No witness gives explicit information about its exemplar.

(*a*) If a witness, J, exhibits all the errors of another surviving witness, F, and in addition at least one error of its own ('peculiar error'), then J must be assumed to derive from F.

Sometimes a witness can be shown to depend on another surviving witness from a single passage, viz., if the peculiar error in the descendant is clearly due to the external state of the text in the surviving exemplar; e.g. where physical damage to the text in the exemplar has caused the loss of letters or groups of letters, and these letters are missing in the descendant without any visible external cause; or where additions claimed as his own by the scribe of the exemplar reappear in the copy without any such indication; or where in copying a prose exemplar a line has been omitted, destroying the logical unity, &c. (cf. p. 43, bottom).

As all copies must be later in date than their exemplars, we can often ascertain which witness is to be treated as the exemplar if we can fix the date of the script in each case.

(*b*) If two witnesses, G and H, show peculiar errors in common as against all the other witnesses, and in addition each shows at least one peculiar error of its own, then both must derive from a common exemplar ϵ, from which the remaining witnesses are not derived. The text of ϵ can be reconstructed

(1) where G and H agree,

(2) where G or H agrees with one of the other witnesses (so peculiar errors of G or H cannot, generally speaking, render the reconstruction of ϵ doubtful).

The text of ϵ is doubtful only where G and H agree neither with each other nor with one of the other witnesses, or if they happen to make the same mistake independently of each other.

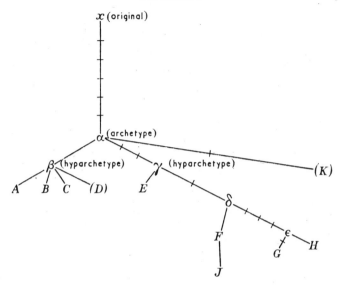

In the same way and with equal certainty the text of δ can be reconstructed on the evidence of F and ε and the text of γ on the evidence of E and δ.

(*c*) If three or more witnesses ABC(D) show peculiar errors in common as against all the rest, and in addition each of the three or more shows peculiar errors of its own, but we never find two of the three (or more) showing common peculiar errors as against the third (or the others), then ABC(D) must, independently of each other, derive from a common source β. The text of β can be reconstructed

(1) where any two of the witnesses ABC(D) agree,

(2) where any one of these witnesses agrees with γ.

The text of β is doubtful only if ABC(D) all disagree with each other and with γ. So all peculiar errors of ABC(D)Eδ (and of course those of FGH also) are, generally speaking, worthless for the reconstruction of β and γ, and must be eliminated (*eliminatio lectionum singularium*).

(*d*) It will be obvious that if any number of further splits in the tradition had occurred after β and γ, the interrelationship of the witnesses, as also the text of β and γ, could be reconstructed with like certainty.

(*e*) The reconstruction of α is a different matter. If its tradition has two branches only, β and γ, and β and γ agree, we have the text of α. If they do not agree, then either of the two readings may be the text of α; we have here *variants*, between which it is not possible to decide on the lines of our procedure hitherto. The *reconstructed variant-carriers* may be called *hyparchetypes*.

(*f*) α could be reconstructed with equal certainty if from each of the branches β and γ only one witness survived, say A and J; A and J would then be the variant-carriers. Still, the position would be considerably worsened if, during the later course of the tradition, further damage had been done to a passage already corrupt in β and γ, or if in a passage corrupt in β but still sound in γ a later corruption appeared in J.

(*g*) The same would be true if, for instance, A, E, and J had alone survived. In that case, where EJ agreed against A, A and γ (= EJ) would be the variant-carriers. If AJ agree against E or AE against J, the isolated readings are worthless (see above). Only when A, J, and E *all* have different readings is it impossible to reconstruct either γ or α by the means so far mentioned. We must then try to arrive at the reading of γ from the '*subvariants*' E and J (see below), so that this may stand as a variant of equal stemmatic value with A.

(*h*) If on the other hand only, e.g., AB or EG or GH had survived, it would only be possible to reconstruct the exemplars β or γ or ϵ, and in that case each of the two surviving witnesses would become a variant-carrier for its exemplar.

(*i*) So far we have found no clue for ascertaining how many steps of the tradition lie between the different points where splits occurred, and how many between the final points of splitting and the surviving witnesses. And if we could find such a clue it would hardly make any difference for the reconstruction of the original (but see (*f*) above).

9. If α has split not merely into β and γ but also into K or still further branches, the text of α is guaranteed by the agreement of two of these branches. Only when all the three (or more) branches disagree or if the agreement between two could be due to both having fallen into the same error independently of each other is the text of α doubtful.

This also applies to the reconstruction of β, if neither γ nor K has survived.

10. If the first of the assumptions made in § 6 does not apply, that is, if individual scribes have 'contaminated' several exemplars, the process of *eliminatio* within the area of these 'contaminations' is greatly hindered, if not made impossible.

Contamination is revealed where the contaminated witness on the one hand fails to show the peculiar errors of its exemplar (having corrected them from another source), and on the other hand *does* exhibit peculiar errors of exemplars on which he does not in the main depend. For instance, suppose there are three witnesses β, γ, and K. If an error is shared sometimes between β and γ against K, sometimes between K and β against γ, and sometimes between K and γ against β, then β, γ, and K are contaminated with each other, and their isolated readings, which would be worthless in ordinary circumstances (see above), all become 'presumptive variants' for the reconstruction of α.

Contamination need not necessarily have come about through a scribe having two exemplars before him and giving now the text of one, now that of the other; this is a very exhausting and, for that reason, unlikely procedure. What has happened is far more likely to have been something like this: in a manuscript, say F, the dissident readings of the other manuscript, which is *not* its exemplar—say A—are noted in the margin or between the lines; J in this case follows now the first reading of F, now the marginal or interlinear reading. If A and F are then lost, we cannot reach a clear picture of the ancestry of J, since J will show some (but not all) of the special errors of β as well as some (but not all) of the special errors of δ.

Some degree of protection against contamination is provided if a work is transmitted in particular branches of the tradition under an altered title, so that the branches of the primary form are isolated from the individual branches of the secondary form. Moreover obvious corruptions, particularly *lacunae*, may easily be transmitted in the direct line but are hardly ever transferred by contamination; so that where peculiar errors of this kind occur it will often be possible to establish with probability the original relation between the witnesses.

11. If the second assumption made in § 6 does not apply, that is, if a scribe does *not* deviate from his exemplar, it is often impossible to establish the relation of the witness to its exemplar and the other descendants of the exemplar. E.g., if F has made no special error in the process of copying from δ, we cannot say whether J depends directly on δ or goes back to δ through F. And if F and J alone survive, then J becomes a presumptive variant-carrier, whereas if we could see through to the true position we should have to eliminate it entirely; so all its special readings must be *examined* (see C below), even though they may in fact all turn out to be peculiar errors. This shows us how vital it may be to find positive proofs of the dependence of a witness on another surviving witness (§ 8*a*, note and cf. Appendix I).

Further untypical instances: if a scribe emends a mistake of his exemplar correctly by conjecture without explicitly stating this, the impression may be conveyed that he depends on another exemplar or has contaminated his text from such an exemplar. Therefore correct readings which could have been reached by conjecture must not be allowed to save a witness from elimination if this is required on other grounds. The task of establishing what readings a witness could or could not have reached by conjecture belongs to the *examinatio* of the presumptive variants (§ 19 *ad fin.*).

12. The interrelationships of the manuscripts of the classics have not as yet, for the most part, been conclusively investigated, quite apart from the numerous instances where contamination makes it impossible to hope for a clear-cut solution.

C. EXAMINATIO

13. The process of *recensio*, then, leads us as a rule either
(1) to a surviving *codex unicus*, or (2) to an archetype which
can be reconstructed with certainty throughout, or (3) to
two variant-carriers which either survive or can be reconstructed; these variant-carriers guarantee the text of the
archetype only when they agree (not of course when they
vary). Disregarding for the moment the latter case (for
which see § 19), we must test the uniform tradition of the
cases where they agree to discover whether it represents the
original.

14. As a result of this *examinatio* we discover that the
tradition is either (1) the best conceivable, or (2) as good
as other conceivable traditions, or (3) worse than another
conceivable tradition but at all events tolerable, or (4)
intolerable.

In the first of these four cases we must look on the tradition as original, in the last as corrupt; in the other two cases
we may, or must, hesitate.

There is, of course, no absolute standard of good or bad
to guide us here; in judging matters of form we must go by
the style of the work, in matters of content by the author's
presumable knowledge or point of view. As regards subject-matter the classical scholar must often turn for help to
other branches of knowledge (technical, &c.); in matters of
style he alone is responsible, and it must be his keenest
endeavour throughout his life to perfect his feeling for style,
even if he realizes that one man's lifetime is not long enough
to allow a real mastery in this field to reach maturity. (Cf.

Wilamowitz, 'Geschichte der Philologie', in Gercke-Norden, *Einleitung in die Altertumswissenschaft*, i (3rd ed.), 1, 49.)

If the archetype of a complete work proves to be entirely free of corruptions, it may be the original, i.e. the split in the tradition may have started with the original. I know no major classical work where this possibility is to be reckoned with, and in shorter works it would not bring us any further.

15. If the tradition proves to be corrupt, we must attempt to remedy it by conjecture (*divinatio*). This attempt leads either to a self-evident emendation or to several more or less equally satisfying conjectures or to the recognition that a cure by conjecture has not been discovered—a crux. The typical conjecture consists in the removal of an anomaly. Now there are some anomalies which were admitted or intended by the author, while others are due to corruption. The assumption then in making a conjecture is that we recognize that an anomaly could not possibly have been admitted or intended by the author. This will be so where we meet with a very harsh anomaly or several smaller anomalies together. But how are we to proceed where the deviation from the normal is comparatively small? In such cases there is room for doubt; but in many the doubt will be removed by the conjecture itself for the following reason. As a rule, no writer will aspire to an anomaly for its own sake; an anomaly is a consequence of his desire to say something out of the ordinary for which the normal mode of expression was found to be inadequate. If we can show that he could, without any sacrifice, have expressed in a normal way what the tradition expresses anomalously, then the anomaly is probably based on a corruption; at the very least the question arises *why* the writer has rejected the

normal, and so long as this question has not been satis-
factorily answered the text remains doubtful. On the other
hand, the great value of many 'superfluous' conjectures lies
in the fact that it is just these which show why the writer
has avoided the normal expression; one would have to
think of these conjectures all over again during the process
of *examinatio* if they were not for the most part there already.
Whether the author of such a conjecture thought 'the
writer *must* have written this' or 'he *ought* to have written
this' is relatively unimportant; the conjecture stimulates
inquiry and often decidedly advances it, and this in the
briefest possible way.

We must distinguish sharply between anomaly and *singularity*.
What is unique is not for that reason alone to be regarded with suspicion.

A text is incurable, or only curable with the aid of a
lucky coincidence (methodically speaking this comes more
or less to the same thing), not only where a reading that is
not abnormal has suffered deep corruption, but often when
a deliberate anomaly or something unusual or unlikely has
suffered only small damage. As it is precisely anomalies,
unique expressions, &c. which are, by their very nature,
peculiarly liable to corruption, and as we can hardly ever
exclude the possibility that something of this kind lies at the
bottom of the difficulty, it will be seen that the impossi-
bility of making a self-evident conjecture ought not to
decide us against presuming a corruption.

16. Where several conjectures are available we should
choose in the first instance that which is best in style
and matter, in the second that which makes it easiest to see

how the corruption arose. In guessing at how the corruption arose we must take into account:

(*a*) what mistakes are most likely to occur on psychological grounds (e.g. the tendency for an uncommon expression to be replaced by a common one, 'trivialization'; this is why it is right to prefer as a rule the '*lectio difficilior*') ;

(*b*) what class of corruption can be shown to exist most frequently in the tradition in question;

(*c*) what sort of corruptions are most likely to have arisen, in the period between original and archetype, on other grounds (history of the tradition of the author involved, history of the transmission of texts in general, history of language, script, orthography, state of classical scholarship, editing technique, cultural conditions, &c.).

The task of proving the existence of the conjecturally (or 'selectionally', see § 19) presupposed errors plays a considerable but always *secondary* role in textual criticism. The opportunity for such a demonstration occurs only where we have several conjectures (or variants) of roughly equal value in style and content to choose from, or where it is a question of choosing between conjecture and crux. The main business, that of determining what is either tolerable or absolutely required from the point of view of style or content, will not be materially advanced by our perceiving what errors are more or less probable. Moreover a reading is by no means necessarily wrong if there is no obvious explanation of the error in the tradition which the reading presupposes. We can know what are the commonest kinds of corruption, but we cannot be sure that a particular corruption belongs to any one of them; corruptions have a way of becoming further corrupted in transmission. We can sometimes be sure that a right reading in a text is right, even if it rests on conjecture; we can scarcely ever be sure that a corruption is one that could not have occurred. In any case experience teaches us that various types of error occur with varying frequency, and therefore have varying degrees of probability in doubtful cases. But we still have no standard for judging which errors are to be regarded as probable in individual cases. The collections of common errors that have been made so far simply give examples of specific types of error which no one has ever denied; they give no picture of the varying frequency of errors and, worse still, they do not show which types of error do *not* occur.

To reach firm ground in this field it would be necessary to prepare a catalogue of all peculiar errors (see § 6), arranged in classes according to the different periods of history, types of literature, and the scripts used in the different localities, using such witnesses as derive from surviving exemplars (in consequence of which their peculiar readings are not normally found in critical editions). One would then have to proceed to the peculiar errors of witnesses whose exemplars can be reconstructed with certainty by *recensio*; only in the last resort should those witnesses be adduced whose exemplars can only be reconstructed by selection (*selectio*) or conjecture (*divinatio*).

An investigation of this kind would be particularly desirable in the case of *interpolations*, i.e. the class of alterations (mostly insertions) which is not due to accident but is an attempt to restore the original or actually to represent forged matter as original, by a conscious but not openly admitted interference with the tradition. Alterations of this kind are particularly dangerous, as it is often very difficult

to prove that a text based on them has been deformed
(whereas scribal blunders normally produce obvious nonsense); and in texts where such an interpolation has been demonstrated much becomes suspect simply because it appears
to be superfluous. And it is so easy simply to cut out what
could easily be dispensed with! But there is undoubtedly
superfluous (or at least not demonstrably indispensable)
matter in every original. So very thorny problems arise.
The history of interpolation is closely linked with that of the
forging of whole works; this too would be worth writing.

If an archetype (or *codex unicus*) is in certain sections
degraded to the rank of a variant-carrier or even of a *codex
descriptus*, mistakes of the kinds which can be demonstrated in
these sections may also be suspected to exist in those sections
where we have no check. Here lies the great value of *citations*,
where they derive from an older branch of the tradition.

On the other hand, one may have to collect and classify
all the peculiar errors of a *codex descriptus* in order to know
what peculiar errors are likely to have occurred in the cases
where it becomes a variant-carrier or the *codex unicus*. Admittedly this will only reveal the latest stratum of errors.

17. In consequence it may sometimes be important to
determine the date of the reconstructed archetype, to save
oneself from having to consider the possibility of corruptions of a kind likely to have occurred only at a date later
than that of the archetype. The archetype must be earlier
than the time of the earliest datable variant (not only than
the earliest datable variant-carrier) and later than the date
of the latest datable corruption.

18. What degree of certainty can we hope to attain in the *examinatio*, particularly in conjecture? A conjecture may be confirmed or at least supported either by the agreement of all persons qualified to judge (admittedly this is not an easy concept to define) or by new arguments not noticed by the originator or by the later appearance of a witness earlier than the archetype (unless the reading of this too is a conjecture). It may be refuted either by showing that the tradition is sound or by means of a better reading due either to conjecture or to the discovery of new witnesses of an earlier tradition. The last few decades have seen an over-abundance of such confirmations and refutations, but we still possess no survey which shows how these could be used to improve our methods. Such a survey would be extremely useful. The new knowledge has splendidly confirmed the acumen of many editors; but the surprises sprung on us by almost every papyrus find, and still more the radical discrepancies in the standard editions where the tradition itself remains unchanged, do not indicate that *examinatio* has brought the texts in general to a very high degree of certainty. All too often, even in the most widely read classical texts, the best-qualified critics had overlooked a corruption, wrongly cast suspicion on a sound tradition, treated a wrong conjecture as a certain restoration of the original, or rejected a correct emendation. The question is whether these mistakes are due merely to insufficient concentration on the individual case (which might be excused in view of the vast extent of the material) or whether we are faced with faults in *method*. My general impression is that on the one hand too many conjectures have been accepted of a kind which assumes a violent (that is, really irremediable) mutilation of the text, while on the other hand scholars have been too ready to overlook corruptions in the tradition or the vulgate text simply because no convincing solution has yet been offered. Both these faults spring from a reprehensible fear of admitting that one has not reached an entirely satisfying solution; for to present what is doubtful as certain is to remain farther from the goal than if one were to confess one's doubt. Admittedly the former procedure takes fewer words, but this is a misleading brevity; it easily tempts others to assert the opposite with equal brevity, and only a third mode of presentation will do justice to the true position (i.e. that the case is doubtful). Of course this is true in all fields of research, and an over-conscientious weighing of probabilities is liable eventually to stifle the germ of progress. But texts are the foundation of all philological investigation and should be so treated that the least possible doubt prevails as to how far they are reliable.

We may just mention the passing aberration of the school which opposed all conjectural criticism on principle. Of course it is far more dangerous for a corruption to pass unrecognized than for a sound text to be unjustifiably attacked. For as every conjecture provokes refutation, this at all events advances our understanding of the passage, and only the best conjectures will win acceptance; on the other hand, the unnoticed corruption damages our total impression of the style, and anyone who fails to recognize a right conjecture lays himself open to the reproach of ingratitude, if not of envy. Anyone who is afraid of giving an uncertain text had best confine himself to dealing with autograph manuscripts.

19. When the tradition splits into *two* branches the process of *recensio* (above, § 13) often leads us to two variants. In the *examinatio*, then, we must establish whether one or neither of these is original.

A typical instance. One of the two variants can be understood as an error, which means that the other variant must
be the reading of the archetype. This reading of the arch-
type, reached by *selectio*, then becomes the basis of further
examinatio.

To decide what type of errors is most likely to be found in a
variant-carrier we proceed on the lines described in § 16, substituting
for 'period between original and archetype' the words 'period between
archetype and variant-carrier'.

Untypical instances. (*a*) Both variants may be understood as
errors stemming from the same reading in the archetype.
This reading of the archetype, discovered by *divinatio* (*com-
binatio*), hereupon becomes the basis of further *examinatio*.

This case is untypical, because it can only occur if a passage which
remained sound up to the time of the archetype (otherwise the reading
of the archetype could not be found by conjecture) has been mutilated
differently in the two branches.

(*b*) No reading can be found which explains both variants.
In this case the reconstruction of the original remains
doubtful, even if the reading of the original arrived at by
selectio or *divinatio* is completely satisfying in style and content and explains how one of the variants arose, since
the variant whose origin remains obscure may go back to a
better reading of the original not yet discovered by conjecture. We must also consider the possibility that there were
two versions of the original; admittedly the two versions
would then have to have been already 'contaminated' in the
archetype.

(*c*) By the side of one variant we have two subvariants
(§ 8*g*). In this case we have in the first instance not three
readings to choose from but two only—that of the surviving
variant-carrier and that of the second variant-carrier which

may be reconstructed from the two sub-variants. The original reading, to be found by selection or conjecture, must in this case be such as to make the existence of the three readings for which witnesses exist comprehensible in terms of the stemmatic relationship established during the process of *recensio*.

However much the two variant-carriers vary in value, the *selectio* must be made independently in each case; no variant should be rejected without testing. After all, in recognizing a witness as a variant-carrier we presuppose that it does not share at least one special error of the other variant-carrier; but if it alone has preserved the original in one passage, we are bound to reckon with the same possibility in all the readings peculiar to it.

The presumptive variants which appear where the relations between the different branches of the tradition have not been cleared up (10, 11) and the variants of a tradition split into three or more branches in the cases where all witnesses diverge (9) must be tested in the same way.

20. These methods of testing variants have now been more or less generally recognized in principle, although only very recently. Previously the principle was to follow the vulgate (*textus receptus*) without troubling about the quality of the witnesses; or to follow the text of the majority of the witnesses, in spite of the fact that 100 manuscripts which derive from a single manuscript have less authority than this single manuscript and have no more authority than one manuscript which does not go back to that single manuscript; or to follow the oldest, the most complete, the best witness, just as if *every* scribe were not liable to error. This was all completely arbitrary, and there was never any attempt made at a methodical justification. The mistake of treating the *codex optimus* as if it were the *codex unicus* has not been completely overcome even today; it is often set right by the *codex optimus* finally revealing itself as the *codex unicus*.

21. The diagram which exhibits the inter-relationship of the witnesses is called the *stemma*. The image is taken from genealogy: the witnesses are related to the original somewhat as the descendants of a man are related to their ancestor. One might perhaps illustrate the transmission of errors along the same lines by treating all females as sources of error. But the essential point, the aim of reconstructing the original, is not brought out by this comparison. The formation of branches on a tree grafted with slips of different species at different points would give a picture of the task of *recensio* and the character of the archetype. The following 'simile' perhaps corresponds more precisely:

A river comes from an inaccessible source under the peak of a high mountain. It divides underground, its branches divide further, and some of these branches then come to the surface on the mountain side as springs; the water of these springs at once drains away and may come to the surface at several places farther down the mountain side and finally flows onward in visible form overground. The water from its source onwards is of ever-changing but fine and pure colours. In its subterranean course it flows past several places at which colouring matters from time to time dissolve into the water; the same thing happens every time the stream divides and every time it comes to the surface in a spring. Every influx changes the colour of a certain part of the stream, and this part keeps the colour permanently; only very slight colour changes are eliminated by natural processes. The distinction between the dyed water and the original remains always visible to the eye, but only occasionally in the sense that the eye at once recognizes a colour as falsified by influxes; often only in the sense that the difference between the colours of the various springs is discernible. On the other hand, the falsified elements can often be detected and the original colour restored by chemical methods; at other times this method fails. The object of the investigation is to test the genuineness of the colours on the evidence of the springs.

22. The methods most closely related to the method of 'stemmatics' are those of historical criticism of sources. But whereas a literary tradition goes back to an original similar in character to all the witnesses, in that it also is a manuscript, an historical tradition begins with an event, which by its very nature resists being set down in literary form, and is misrepresented or falsified, often even consciously, by the earliest witnesses. A work of literary art is an organic whole, and the reader is conscious of each element as standing in a necessary relation to every other element in it; it can survive over thousands of years without suffering serious damage, particularly in a civilization susceptible to its effect. But of the historical event often only the roughest outlines, and sometimes not even these, are free from doubt.

It is useful also to compare the methods of archaeology, which reconstructs a lost work of art from its copies, or those of literary or folk-lore research, which looks for the original version of a motif. But nowhere will the road be so clear, the goal so certainly attainable, as in the textual criticism of the classical authors.

D. BEARING OF THESE ARGUMENTS ON THE PREPARATION OF A CRITICAL EDITION

23. The preface should (1) describe all witnesses, the main witnesses (*codices unici*, variant-carriers) of course in most detail, but not omit even those eventually to be discarded, or those only to be considered for a few passages, (2) demonstrate the relationship of the witnesses where this is at all possible in a *stemma*, proving each connexion by adducing a number of characteristic peculiar errors, (3) characterize the quality of the archetype and variant-carriers by assembling the corruptions by classes, (4) settle all questions of spelling and dialect.

In the text the following signs should be used:

for conjectural additions ⟨ ⟩
for conjectural deletions ⟦ ⟧ or { }
for supplements in the case of physical damage [ ]
for irremediable corruptions (where these can be localized) †.

In Latin texts conjectural changes of words or parts of words may be indicated in italics.

The distinction between [ ] and ⟨ ⟩ is important. ⟨ ⟩ intimates that the very assumption that a lacuna exists is conjectural, while [ ] shows that a lacuna of known length has been filled up. [ ] should also be used where the tradition explicitly notes that the exemplar contained a lacuna.

Where the manuscripts have not suffered physical damage, [ ] may also be used to mark deletions.

Underneath the text the following should be noted:

(1) Every departure from the archetype not already indicated in the text.

(2) All rejected variants (even scribal errors); not that these affect the constitution of the text, but to indicate to the reader that at this point the text is based not on the archetype but on a later stage of the tradition.

(3) The sub-variants, where they are not to be eliminated.

(4) Identical readings of two or more variant-carriers, if they are rejected in favour of the reading of a further

variant-carrier. If a reading adopted from a variant-carrier must be regarded as a conjecture, it should be marked as such.

(5) Doubt as to the correctness of the text.

The *apparatus criticus* is placed underneath the text simply on account of bookprinting conditions and in particular of the format of modern books. The practice in ancient and medieval manuscripts of using the outer margin for this purpose makes for far greater clarity. This might be attempted in printing in specially suitable cases, e.g., in Greek tragedy; of course, for the more important notes only.

24. Where the witnesses change (i.e., where important branches of the tradition enter or are withdrawn for a section) these changes must be accounted for on the page, between the text and the apparatus. If the change means that the archetype is replaced by an earlier witness, then for this section the former archetype is classed as a variant-carrier or even lower and must be treated in the *apparatus* accordingly (sub-variants to be eliminated, &c.). If the former archetype is replaced by a later witness (where one variant-carrier ceases to be available), then in view of the new circumstances the readings of the witnesses eliminated up till now must be inserted.

Readings which must quite certainly be eliminated have no place under the text. Presumptive variants are best assembled in an appendix.

If rejected variants, 'combinations', or conjectures of roughly equal value to those adopted exist, attention should be called to them by italicizing or by the note, '*fortasse recte*'.

It is the practice to indicate the authorship of conjectures. But justice and consistency demand that mention should also be made of the scholar who first explained the transmitted text or pointed out the corruption. In both cases a selection only need be given; on the other hand at times a brief justification of the course taken should be offered, e.g. changes made purely *metri causa* should be indicated and marked as such. Our present *apparatus critici* have too little life in them.

Once the text has been constituted on the basis of *recensio* and *examinatio* it must be elucidated by the separation of words, marking of pauses, colometry, stops, initial capitals, &c. This certainly comes within the sphere of a critical edition, but it belongs to *interpretatio*, the aims of which change with changing times and in any case cannot be standardized like those of textual criticism.

E. EXAMPLES

25. *Documentation* (cf. §§ 3 ff.). The *codices unici* of the classics and the most important variant-carriers (see § 19) have, on the whole, been adequately described and collated. Many of them are available in photographic facsimiles, which are sometimes easier to decipher than the originals. Still, it is not always possible to dispense with the original where decisions have to be made on the make-up of the manuscripts, erasures, differences in ink, paper, &c. Even in the most-read texts one can occasionally find details unnoticed; e.g. in Aesch. *Septem* 915 the *scholium* in the Mediceus reads προπομποί not προπομπά, a reading which is not without importance for the text of the poet. In Plato, *Meno* 99 e, all the manuscripts give after οὐδὲν μέλει ἔμοιγε the sign for change of speaker, thus confirming Wilamowitz's conjecture that these words are not spoken by Socrates. Many readings in the Medicean manuscripts of Tacitus were deciphered for the first time by G. Andresen. On Theocritus 15. 72 Ziegler gives in his edition of 1879, p. 190, a facsimile of the reading of the variant-carrier K; it is not ἄθρεως but ἀθέως, and this is confirmed by *Pap. Oxy.* 1618, which offers the correct reading, ἀλαθέως. [There are still no accessible photographs of many papyri which are *testes unici* for important classical texts, and there are many papyri whose present location is not published. 1949].

First editions of texts based on a *codex unicus* not easy to decipher rarely allow of a conclusive transcription. It has often been possible to make further headway simply on the basis of examples of the script furnished by the editor, or even by conjecture alone without knowledge of the script (e.g. in the case of the Cairo MS. of Menander). On the other hand the objectivity of a collation can easily be endangered by unconscious conjecture. The most reliable collator is the man who (1) best understands the text, (2) is able to 'switch off' his knowledge and work purely visually. The charred remnants of the papyri from Herculaneum demand a scholar who is at the same time a skilled draftsman. [Altogether too little use is made of drawing in preparing first editions of mutilated texts. 1949.] On the treatment of palimpsests compare my *Griechische Paläographie* (Gercke–Norden, *Einleitung in die Alterumswissenschaft*, i (3rd ed.), 9. 9). Only in exceptional instances have palaeographical methods had to be used to detect modern forgeries (cf. E. Norden, *Die römische Literatur* in Gercke–Norden, op. cit. 4. 100 and *Sitzungsber. der Berlin. Akad.* 1924, 163).

26. *Intermediate offshoots with change of title* (§ 10). (1) The tradition of the Codex Theodosianus, which has general importance as an example because several branches can be dated (stemma to be found in *Göttingische Gelehrte Anzeiger*, 1906, 643). (2) The tradition of some of the *Letters* of Gregory of Nyssa (ed. Pasquali, 1925. Note on p. 82, 15, cf.

p. lxiii; how can a single manuscript of the forged Libanius letters have preserved a variant of the Gregory tradition, unless this stood in the archetype of the Libanius letters?).

27. *Presumptive variants* (§ 11). For the nine plays of Euripides which lack scholia (*Hel.*, *El.*, *Heracl.*, *Herc.*, *Suppl.*, *I.T.*, *I.A.*, *Ion*, *Cycl.*) there are two manuscripts only, of which the first, L (*saec.* xiii–xiv) has very few, the second P (*saec.* xiv–xv) a great number of peculiar errors. This leads to the conjecture that P derives from L. If this is so, wherever P has the better reading, this must come from a conjecture of the fourteenth century. The most important three passages are these from the *I.T.*:

1005   . . . οὐ γὰρ ἀλλ' ἀνὴρ μὲν ἐκ δόμων
θανὼν ποθεινός, τὰ δὲ γυναικὸς ἀσθενῆ.

This is the reading of P; L reads γυναικῶν with a violation of Porson's Law quite impossible for Euripides. Now there is no evidence that anyone between Seneca and Porson knew this law; but there is nothing to prevent us from presuming that some Byzantine correctly restored the singular for the sake of symmetry; cf. the deliberate alteration of the text in P at 839.

1441 a   ἄγαλμα θ' ἱερὸν εἰς ἐμὴν ἄξων χθόνα
1441 b   τῶν νῦν παρόντων πημάτων ἀναψυχάς.

The second verse is missing in P; but it is so disturbing and superfluous at first sight that any thinking reader could probably have struck it out. In any case this athetization suits better with the peculiar errors of P than interpolation suits with the peculiar errors of L. However, the line may be genuine (cf. 92 and *Ion* 1604, another speech of Athena *ex*

machina, and the play is of about the same date; *Hipp.* 600;
[Soph.] fr. 1025. 5 πημάτων παραψυχὰς | θεῶν ἀγάλματα).

692 . . . λήγειν βίον.

This is the reading of L, corrected from λήσειν; P reads
λύσειν. Some scholars have held that the original read
λύειν or λῦσαι, overlooking the fact that λήγειν transitive
recurs at *Ion* 1404 and deserves preference as the *lectio
difficilior*.

No reading of P has so far been produced which cannot
derive from L. Of course this does not suffice to prove that
P does in fact descend from L. L could have made just those
few errors in copying from an exemplar common to both L
and P. But in the first place this would be most unlikely in a
text of such length, and secondly there are several errors in
P which can only be explained as misreadings of passages
not clearly written in L (as shown by N. Wecklein; on this
see *Gnomon*, ii (1926), 156). This means that we can really
eliminate P, and this has been done in the Collection Budé
edition of Euripides.

28. *Gaps in our knowledge of the manuscripts* (§ 12). In
principle we should insist that no witness be eliminated
until it has been established that it depends exclusively on
surviving exemplars or on exemplars which can be reconstructed without its help, i.e. until all its peculiar readings
have been tested. But in extensive texts, where a large
number of witnesses exist, obedience to this principle would
involve an enormous amount of labour which might on
occasion produce practically no improvement in the text
and whose results would be far too expensive to publish.
So we shall often have to make shift for the time being—

establishing the stemmatic position only roughly, eliminating witnesses after testing samples (in cases where peculiar errors are shared with surviving or reconstructible witnesses), and allowing only the variant-carriers to be fully represented. Even so the information provided at the present stage of our knowledge is far from being as complete as it should be. Only one branch of the two-branched tradition of the Βιβλιοθήκη of Photius has been made available. In the traditions of Theognis [cf. now D. C. C. Young, *Scriptorium*, vii (1953), 3 ff.], Sophocles, Aristophanes, Plato, Apollonius Rhodius, Lucretius, and Lucan the stemmatic relationships of important branches have not yet been investigated. There is a thirteenth-century manuscript of Strabo on Mount Athos (Vatopedi) which has not so far been made use of. Citations deriving from a branch of the tradition earlier than the archetype have indeed in most cases been investigated to discover whether they offer improvements in the text. But they are still often not treated throughout (as they deserve to be) as variant-carriers for the reconstruction of the earlier archetype which could be reached with their aid.

29. *Removal of a harsh anomaly* (§ 15). In Sappho fr. 96. 8 L.P. the tradition has μήνα, where the metre requires ∪ − −; the synonym σελάννα satisfies this requirement. Anyone who believes it possible that Sappho nevertheless wrote μήνα would have to believe that a modern poet, in a poem otherwise rhyming throughout, would be capable of rhyming 'night' not with 'delight' but with 'joy'.

30. *Removal of an accumulation of several minor difficulties* (§ 15). In Call. *Hymn.* 4. 226 f. Iris has to report to Hera that she has not been able to prevent Asteria (= Delos) from granting Leto a haven for her confinement. Her speech ends thus

νεο   ους

ἀλλὰ φίλη (δύνασαι γάρ) ἀμύνειν πότνια δούλοις

ους   τμήν.

ὑμετέροις, οἳ σεῖο πέδον πατέουσιν ἐφετμῇ.

(the transmitted text, with conjectures inserted above)

Difficulties in the transmitted text

1. Iris' request for help is out of place here; it is too late for help, in fact she returns only *because* her task is completed. Nor is there any further mention of an attempt to interfere with the confinement.

2. The infinitive with imperatival force after parenthetical δύνασαι is almost intolerably harsh.

3. ἀμύνειν violates the bucolic diaeresis (see below, § 31); the fact that the *Iliad* has ἀμύνειν several times among several hundred lines which offend against this rule proves nothing for Callimachus.

4. 'Tread the ground' is a bad way of expressing the function of the winged messenger of the gods.

Improved text

1. Iris is seeking to ward off Hera's anger from herself (cf. 217 φόβῳ), by demanding the punishment of Asteria; Hera magnanimously refuses to exact punishment. All this makes excellent sense.

2. The imitations in Agath. *Anth. Pal.* 6. 7 ἀλλὰ θεά (δύνασαι γὰρ) . . . τεῦχε and Paul. Silent. *Ecphr.* 224 ἀλλὰ μάκαρ (δύνασαι γὰρ . . . πάσσειν) . . . προτίταινε support the imperative.

3. ἀμύνεο is metrically blameless. The corruption was made easier by the preceding δύνασαι.

4. 'Those who trample underfoot thy command' (not to receive Leto, cf. 203) is an excellent way of designating Asteria's guilt.

5. πέδον πατεῖν in the sense of γαῖαν πατεῖν (Theocr. 18. 20) is unexampled ['but cf. Gregor. Nazianz. *carm.* ii. 1. 13. 122 in *Patrolog. Gr.* xxxvii (1237)'. R. Pfeiffer in a private letter. 1949].

5. πέδον πατεῖν in the sense of λακπατεῖν occurs in Aesch. *Ag.* 1357, *Choeph.* 643 (no further attempts should now be made to alter this). πατεῖν occurs in a similar sense in Call. a few lines farther on (248).

What makes this fourfold alteration convincing is the fact that in the attempt at restoring the appropriate sense the metrical, the syntactical, and the lexicographical difficulties disappear of themselves and there comes to light an archaic expression (πέδον πατεῖν) the almost inevitable misunderstanding of which was practically bound to lead to the corruption: anyone who took πέδον as accusative object of πατεῖν would have to change ἐφετμήν (probably written ἐφετμῇ, cf. 195, 298, &c.) to ἐφετμῇ, then make the δοῦλοι refer to Iris, and then convert 'punish' into 'help', a change made easier by the accident that the root ἀμυν- has both meanings. [The change might have been made in the circle of Michael Choniatas (twelfth century); cf. Pfeiffer's ed. of Callimachus, vol. i (1949) on fr. 251 f., 264, and p. 499 on fr. 1. 1, 7. 30. On the conjectural criticism of the Byzantines cf. *Byz. Zeitschr.* (1936), 27 ff. 1949.]

A glance back at the stages of this discovery may be instructive. Of the five difficulties in the transmitted text the second was first felt by A. Dacier (about 1700), the third by Wordsworth (1844); herein lies the worth of their conjectures (given by O. Schneider), which we need not now quote. I myself published ἀμύνεο (leaving the rest as transmitted) in 1921 (*Neue Responsionsfreiheiten*, part II, 18[2]) but Wilamowitz rightly objected that the middle voice does not give the meaning 'help'. So I tried what could be done with the idea of 'punish', but was then unable to fit in the relative clause. I was discussing this with W. Crönert when he suggested the vital ἐφετμήν (1922, published in 1923 in my *Griechische Metrik* [Gercke–Norden, *Einleitung*, i (3rd ed.), 7] § 92), and it only then became obvious that the transmitted text offered three further difficulties (1, 4, 5), which we had removed without having noticed them. An attractive parallel, Diphilus in Plautus *Rud.* 697 *illos scelestos qui tuum fecerunt fanum parvi fac ut ulciscare*, was pointed out to me in 1925 by Eduard Fraenkel.

31. *Removal of a repeated anomaly.* To supplement the preceding example I may mention one or two other instances where the observation of the bucolic diaeresis leads to an improvement in text.

Call. *Hymn.* 6. 129   ποτὶ τὰν θεῦν ἄχρις ὁμαρτεῖν.

Callimachus uses θεύς once at the end of the verse (6. 57), where the use of the monosyllable is governed by special considerations (see my *Griechische Metrik*, Nachtrag zu § 96); elsewhere he always uses the open forms. This is required here also, and the text has read θεόν (restored in a Renaissance manuscript) since Meineke. The corruption comes from a reminiscence of v. 57, just as in *Hymn.* 5. 138 τὤργον was corrupted into τὤργος because of 54. Here, as often where we are dealing with a *learned* tradition, we must abandon the *lectio difficilior*, which is normally to be preferred.

On Call. 43. 14 Pfeiffer (where there is a stylistic anomaly in addition to the metrical anomaly, which is heightened by the punctuation), see my *Griechische Metrik*, § 139. παραχρῆμα is an ancient explanation (gloss) on the correct reading παρὰ χρέος (Naeke [since confirmed by Pap. Oxy. 2080. 1949]).

Call. fr. 618 Pf. Ῥήγιον ἄστυ λιπὼν ᾿Ιοκάστου Αἰολίδαο.

If this were the reading of all the manuscripts, as Schneider believed, we should hardly know what to do in face of the reading ᾿Ιοκάστου, in spite of the additional difficulty of the anomalous hiatus. In fact this is only the reading of Tzetzes and a scholium on the Odyssey which depends on Tzetzes. The scholia on Dionysius Periegeta 461, 476, on which Tzetzes depends, read ᾿Ιοκάστεω (so also Codex Laur. 28. 25; information kindly supplied by G. Pasquali) or ᾿Ιοκά-στεως, -τεος (according to Bernhardy). Clearly Tzetzes has vulgarized the termination, just as he writes again in Call. *Hymn.* 3. 234 Ἀχαιῶν for Ἀχαιῖδες with the same metrical error. ᾿Ιοκάστεω, already conjectured by Nauck (*Philol.* v. 590, note) is guaranteed by the genitives Δασκύλεω and Σιμύλεω in contemporary Alexandrians (*Anth. Pal.* 7. 709; 6. 34). It is true that objections have been made against this Δασκύλεω on historical grounds. But none of them is of any great weight, and the admirable tradition (Plutarch, Meleager, so probably that of the Alexandrian Library of the second century B.C.) does not encourage any deeper intervention without compelling reasons.

It turns out, then, that Callimachus observed the rule of the bucolic diaeresis without any exceptions; this is known to be true of most poets after Archilochus with any claim to technical competence (cf. my *Griechische Metrik*², 1929, 33 f.). This absence of exception authorizes in some sort

those attempts at emendation undertaken to secure con-
formity to the rule, since it was arrived at without doing
any violence to the transmitted texts. It is particularly
fortunate that all the changes made were also necessary for
other reasons, apart from this rule; the rule would in any
case be valid enough to justify such alterations, even if its
universal application could not be demonstrated. Generally
speaking, we should not over-estimate such an absence of
exceptions to a rule, if only because the material of which
it can be shown to be true is a mere fragment of that
originally existing. Thus there must often remain a slight
element of doubt, but after all, this is not without its fascina-
tion. (The principles for the treatment of metrical anomalies
are discussed by P. Maas, *Neue Responsionsfreiheiten*, i (1914),
§§ 2–5; A. E. Housman, *C.Q.* 1927, 1.)

The tendency towards linguistic consistency can be made
use of in textual criticism in the same way as that towards
metrical consistency, especially where a linguistic standard
attested in extensive texts of uniform quality is guaranteed
on the one hand by the metre, on the other by contemporary
inscriptions, as in the dialogue parts of fifth-century Attic
drama. A survey of the extent and limitations of this consistency, to be used with the collections of O. Lautensach
(1916–21, mostly in *Glotta*), would be most valuable. Over-
estimation of the degree of consistency prevailing has led
to an attempt to discredit the imperatives in -τωσαν and the
optatives in -ημεν (Eur. *Ion* 1131, *I.T.* 1480, *Ion* 943, *Hel.*
1010, *Cycl.* 132, Soph. *Euryp.* fr. 222. 7 P., cf. trag. anon.
PSI 2. 136).

32. *'Singularities' obscured by corruption* (§ 15). Call. fr.

191. 10 Pf. where the tradition has χάλκε(ι)ον instead of Παγχαῖον (corr. R. Bentley, arguing from the traditions concerning Euhemerus, confirmed by the papyrus).

Cercidas fr. 1. 30 Diehl, where the papyrus reads καιαγαθαμεταιδως (with the scholium ἐπεὶ δὼς ἀγαθή, Hesiod *Op*. 356) instead of καὶ Μετάδως (corr. Wilamowitz in the first edition; αγαθα crept into the text from the scholium which was also in the exemplar).

Plaut. *Most.* 1149, where the tradition has *dephilo aut philomontes* for *Diphilo aut Philemoni es* (corr. Leo and Bücheler, *Herm.* 1883, 560).

Varro Atac. fr. 7 Morel, where the tradition has *expedita* for *experdita* (corr. Bücheler, *Jahrb. für Phil.* 1866, 610; the redundant *ex* is attested as a solecism by the grammarians who cite it).

Cicero *in Pison.* 85, where the tradition has *Iovis velsuri* for *Svelsurdi* (corr. J. H. Mordtmann, *Rev. Arch.* 1878, ii, arguing from Thracian inscriptions).

[πατρίδα τὴν αἱρετὴν (ἀρετὴν codd.: corr. K. Hude, 1912) ἡγησάμενοι, says the Athenian-by-choice Lysias (*Epitaph.* § 66) of the metics who fell in the cause of Athenian liberty. 1949.]

Everywhere the possibility of an emendation depends on a lucky coincidence; but it is only the properly equipped scholar who can grasp it. The reader should study Bentley's first essay, the *Epistula ad Millium* (1691), the *incunabulum* of conjectural criticism. Admittedly it offers no guidance as to method.

33. *Interpolations* (§ 16). It will suffice to refer to the text of Homer, that of the jurists in Justinian's *Digests*, and to

Horace *Od.* 4. 8. 14–17 and 3. 11. 17–20. The deletion
of the geographical excursuses in Caes. *Bell. Gall.* (there is
one as early as 1. 1. 5–7) seems certain to be right, although
the numerous difficulties were not noticed until very late
(H. Meusel and A. Klotz, 1910; cf. E. Norden, *Die römische
Literatur* [Gercke-Norden, i (3rd ed.), 4], 107). A particularly
mischievous interpolation in Lucan 7. 388 was very acutely
unmasked by A. E. Housman with the aid of the presumptive variant *explicat* 387 and the emendation *non⟨a⟩ aetas*
made possible by Juv. 13. 28 (cf. Tac. *Ann.* 11. 11).

[G. Jachmann has made the detection of interpolations
the main object of his activity since 1935; cf. H. Fuchs,
Mus. Helv. iv (1948), 190 f., also 164 f. For the text of
Herodotus cf. J. E. Powell in the appendix to his English
translation. 1949.]

[*Forgeries of whole works* (§ 16). Bentley's unmasking of the
Letters of Phalaris in 1699 was an epoch-making achievement.
But the last fifty years have seen the acceptance as genuine
of many a long-rejected text: several of the Letters of Plato,
the *Epitaphioi* of Demosthenes and Lysias, the Letter of
Speusippus to Philip are gradually being recognized as
genuine. The battle is still raging over Euripides' *Rhesus*
and Seneca's *Octavia*. H. Fuchs, in *Mus. Helv.* iv (1948),
188 f., seems to me too sceptical of the tradition. 1949.]

34. *Dating the archetype* (§ 17). A certain *terminus post quem*
for the archetype is supplied, e.g., by such corruptions as
can only be explained as due to misreading of a minuscule
exemplar; e.g. the confusion of $\beta \, \eta \, \kappa \, \mu$. Such an archetype
must be later than the eighth century (e.g. καρύδικος for
βαρύδικος in Aesch. *Choeph.* 936; νεκρόν for νεβρόν *Eum.*

246). A *terminus ante quem* is supplied e.g., by variants which can only have arisen from misreadings of majuscule script ($A \Delta \Lambda$, $\in O \Theta C$), so ἔχεται ἆ for σχέτλια in F at Plato, *Gorg.* 467 b 10; the archetype of BTF must then be earlier than the ninth century. On the other hand majuscule corruptions in the archetype and minuscule corruptions in variant-carriers prove nothing as to the age of the archetype.

35. *Ancient corruptions.* Of course the antiquity of a suspect reading is not in itself an argument against assuming corruption. In Plato, *Symp.* 208 b, the Byzantines and the papyrus both read ἀθάνατον; Creuzer's emendation ἀδύνατον is self-evident. In Timotheus, *Pers.* 234, the papyrus (fourth century B.C.) reads ποικιλομουσοσορινσον; Wilamowitz in the first edition reads ποικιλόμουσον Ὀρφεὺς χέλυν.

The verse Bacchyl. 17. 63 is missing in one of the papyri (O) and is misplaced in the other (A). It must therefore have been added in the margin of the archetype without a clear indication of its right position (Blass had recognized this, on the strength of A, before O was discovered, and at the same time established, and rectified, the omission of a syllable in A, v. 62, which was similarly confirmed by O; Jebb had allowed himself to be convinced by Blass's arguments, others had not). The archetype is doubtless to be placed in Alexandria, about A.D. 100.

36. *Corruption excluded by the quality of the witnesses.* At Vergil *Ecl.* 4. 62, where the manuscripts offer

> *cui non risere parentes*
> *nec deus hunc mensa, dea nec dignata cubili est,*

Quintilian read (9. 3) *qui non risere* and was puzzled at this being followed by *hunc* in the singular. He would hardly have acted so if a variant *cui non risere* had existed at the time; this variant must therefore be disregarded for the process of *recensio*. But *parentes* is nonsense after *qui*, and J. Schrader's conjecture *parenti* (= *parentei* L. Havet) is convincing. The fact that the Quintilian manuscripts also write *cui* and *parentes* is presumably due to contamination from the corrupted Vergil tradition. One will see why Vergil did not write *hos* if one thinks of the 'goddess's couch'; the graecizing (cf. Eur. *Hec.* 195 ὅσοι ἔχουσι ... ῥύεται) of the construction, which in Latin is anomalous, and the whole turn of the phrase of the closing verse are meant to remind one of Theocritus 9 (the man who escaped Circe's spell shared bed and board with her). The latest and most decided champion of this reading is E. Norden, *Geburt des Kindes* (1924), 61 ff.

On the other hand, we must conclude from the corrupt form in which Aristophanes, *Pax* 603 ff., is cited by Diodor. 12. 40. 6 and Aristodemus *Fr. Gr. Hist.* 104 fr. 16 that neither of them took the quotation from Ephorus (*Fr. Gr. Hist.* 70 fr. 196); besides, the contamination with Archilochus (v. 603) presupposes a learned commentary as archetype. The corruption in v. 605 recurs in our manuscripts, and must therefore date from before the Christian era; it has not been convincingly emended (the latest conjecture is Théodore Reinach's ἦρξε λύπης).

37. *Deceptive confirmation.* Plato, *Phaedr.* 245 c, ἀεικίνητον MSS., Cicero (*de re publ.* 6. 27 *quod semper movetur*), Hermogenes (251. 16 R.), Hermeias, Simplicius (*Comm. Arist.* xi. 32. 10), Stobaeus; αὐτοκίνητον (as conjectured by several scholars) Pap. Oxy. 1017 (publ. 1910) of the second century

A.D. (with variant ἀεικίνητον); αὐτοκίνητον was then adopted
by several scholars. The necessity of ἀεικίνητον will become
clear if, disregarding the editions, one places a full stop
after ἀθάνατον 245 c 5 and a semicolon after ζωῆς c 7; the
idea, if not the word, seems moreover to have stood in
Plato's Pythagorean source (*Vorsokr.* 14 A 12; cf. 32 B 21
Diels, Ocellus fr. 1 Harder). The faulty sentence-con-
nexion, to which Plato's careless connexion τὸ δ' ἄλλο κινοῦν
(instead of something like τὸ μὲν οὖν . . .) was a temptation,
is no doubt responsible for the corruption. Moreover the
new witness is considerably later than the archetype, which
could be reconstructed without it; and as there are no
grounds for deriving it from an earlier offshoot, it should
have been eliminated as a *lectio singularis* (§ 8 c). But the
merit of the conjecture remains—it served to indicate a
defect in the *examinatio*.

38. *Confirmation of the difficulty, but not of the emendation.* At
Plato, *Symp.* 204 b the unconstruable ἄν was altered to αὖ or
δή. The papyrus reads ἄν εἴη, and in fact the most likely
scribal error is the omission of some words. At 209 d Ast
and Badham had objected to the construction; the papyrus
sets it right by introducing εἰς before Ἡσίοδον (after Ἡσίοδον insert with Rückert a comma; this might have led us to
the second εἰς). At 213 b Badham objected to ὡς ἐκεῖνον καθ-
ίζειν, the papyrus produced the true reading with κατιδ[εῖν];
doubtless the Byzantine archetype had καθιδεῖν, a common
spelling. The deletion of the three words was an error in
method, as such interpolations are not usual in the narra-
tive portions of Plato. At 219 c καίπερ ἐκεῖνό γε ᾤμην τι
εἶναι was seen by Hug to be grammatically impossible.

Conjecture could scarcely have led to the singular καὶ περὶ ἐκεῖνο of the papyrus, but we could have rested content with obelization.

At Xen. *Symp.* 8. 8 the tradition has ἐρωμένου instead of 'lover', hence ἐραστοῦ (Mosche). The papyrus (*Aegyptus*, 1923, 41) produced ἐρῶ(ν)τος, which could have been envisaged as a conjecture of equal worth.

Catullus 64. 324 (the Parcae are addressing Peleus at his wedding) has

> *Emathiae tutamen opis, c⟨l⟩arissime nato* (Renaissance conjecture).

This was supposed to be an allusion to the as yet nonexistent Achilles! If this had been marked as a crux, the true reading would certainly have been found before A. E. Housman (*C.Q.* 1915, 229); admittedly it was far from obvious, in spite of being the transmitted reading: *Opis carissime nato* = Διίφιλε.

39. *Unnoticed corruption.* Plato *Symp.* 201 d has ὦ φιλούμενε Ἀγάθων. Pap. Oxy. 843 of the *saec.* 2 A.D. (publ. 1907) produced the reading φίλε. No one had noticed that φιλούμενος = φίλος is singular. It is true the corruption remains unexplained. 203 b εἰσελθών: the papyrus has the correct ἐξελθών. 219 d καρτερίαν = 'self-control'; the papyrus produced the appropriate expression ἐγκράτειαν (cf. Arist. *Eth. Nic.* 1150ᵃ37). 223 b εἰς τὸ ἄντικρυς: it was only the papyrus, reading εἴσω ἄντικρυς, which showed how incomprehensible this was. The papyrus improves the text at several other places, where interference would hardly have been justifiable previously; e.g. at 204 c εἶναι before (instead of after) Ἔρωτα, and at 210 a καὶ σὺ before ἔπεσθαι.

40. *Unexpected confirmation of apparently over-daring conjectures.* Menander (*Epitrep.* 388) in Stobaeus 73. 40 = fr. 564 Kock:

> . . . ὁ κακοδαίμων προσδοκῶν
> χάριν παρὰ γυναικὸς κομιεῖσθαι· μὴ μόνον
> κακόν τι προσλάβοιμι.

Bothe and Cobet had each independently transposed κομι-εῖσθαι παρὰ γυναικός, which makes the metre somewhat smoother (a more normal caesura, a more normal resolution παρα for -ρα γυ-). No one had followed them and I fear no one would even today, had not the papyrus confirmed their conjecture. Yet the transmitted text ought to have been suspect so long as it was not clear why Menander had chosen the harsher rhythm where there was no necessity for it.

Nonnus, *Dion.* 15. 112, in the twelfth-century manuscript:

> ἀκροκόμου Φοίνικος ἢ εὐώδινος Ἀθήνης
> ῥιπίζων ἀνέμοισιν ἕλιξ ἐπεσύρισεν ὄρπηξ.

ἐλαίης for Ἀθήνης was conjectured by Koechly, who was not himself convinced by it; it appears in the papyrus. The Nonnus tradition is full of such permutations (the corruption comes from a reminiscence of εὐώδινες Ἀθῆναι 47. 4, 372).

[An improvement in the text of St. Matthew 6. 28 πῶς οὐ ξαίνουσιν οὐδὲ νήθουσιν, as surprising as it is convincing, comes from the reading, discovered in 1938, of the first hand of the Codex Sinaiticus. Cf. T. C. Skeat, *Zeitschr. für neutest. Wiss.* 37. 211 and E. Lobel, *Pap. Oxy.*, Part xix (1948), 60, Note 1. 1949.]

Here I must close. I realize that the selection and arrangement of these examples is arbitrary. But the core of practically every problem in textual criticism is a problem of *style*, and the categories of stylistics are still far less settled than those of textual criticism. And there is the further danger that the editor in making his recension may fall into the habit of forgetting his responsibility for being continually alive to the author's style. Here I may be allowed to end by recalling a remark of Richard Bentley's in his note on Horace, *Odes* 3. 27. 15, *nobis et ratio et res ipsa centum codicibus potiores sunt*. This remark has always tempted some scholars to misuse it, and it will always continue to do so; but it is true.

APPENDIX I

INDICATIVE ERRORS AND STEMMATIC TYPES

ERRORS arising in the course of transcription are of decisive significance in the study of the interrelationships of manuscripts—I may be allowed to use the term 'stemmatics'. Hitherto investigations of errors have been mainly concerned with how they arise and how they can be removed. In what follows I mean to ask simply what characteristics an error must have in order to be utilized for stemmatic purposes, and how many of these errors are required to prove the main types of stemma.

In geology those fossils which are characteristic of certain epochs of the earth's history are denoted in German by the technical term *Leitfossilien* (index fossils); I have similarly employed the term *Leitfehler* (indicative errors, *errores significativi*) for errors which can be utilized to make stemmatic inferences (*Gnomon*, vi (1930), 561).

The dependence of one witness on another cannot, as a rule, be demonstrated directly, but only by excluding the possibility of its being independent. As a rule we can only prove directly (1) that one witness is independent of another, (2) that two witnesses belong together as against a third witness.

We can prove that a witness (B) is independent of another witness (A) by finding in A as against B an error so constituted that our knowledge of the state of conjectural criticism in the period between A and B enables us to feel confident that it cannot have been removed by conjecture during that period. Errors of this kind may be called 'separative errors' (*errores separativi*).

For the state of conjectural criticism in Byzantine times cf. *Byz*.

Zeitschr. xxxvi. 27 ff.; we still have no corresponding investigations for the Latin Middle Ages.

The best-known separative error in the tradition of the Greek classics is probably the omission of the verse Soph. *O.T.* 800 in Cod. Laur. 32. 9 of the tenth or eleventh century (L) as against the thirteenth century manuscripts (AΓ). It is generally agreed today, quite rightly, that no Byzantine in those three centuries, in fact no scholar of any period, could have composed this line. Moreover it has meanwhile been proved by means of other separative errors in L (mostly, it is true, in the text of the scholia) that a number of Byzantine manuscripts of Sophocles are independent of L (cf. *Byz. Zeitschr.* xxxvi. 455 on V. de Marco). The text of the poet in the common exemplar was obviously transcribed by L with unusual care.

It can be proved that two witnesses (B and C) belong together as against a third (A) by showing an error common to B and C of such a nature that it is highly improbable that B and C committed it independently of each other. Such errors may be called 'conjunctive errors' (*errores coniunctivi*).

'Highly improbable' because we cannot always theoretically exclude the possibility of several witnesses independently making the same error. The probability of two witnesses belonging together is the greater, the less often the same error or a similar one occurs in the rest of the text of B or C or of both. For instance, if both witnesses are full of errors due to itacism and the only error they have in common is due to itacism, then nothing is proved for the stemma; if, on the other hand, both witnesses are orthographically sound, one common error caused by itacism makes it likely that they belong together.

These two types of indicative error occur very frequently in extensive texts, so that the two types of relationship mentioned can usually be demonstrated beyond a doubt.

There is another type of indicative error which directly demonstrates the dependence of one witness on another (cf. above § 8 (*a*)). But such errors are so rare or at least so rarely demonstrable that we cannot rely on being able to find one to establish every stemmatic relationship. I therefore leave this type of error out of account in what follows.

Let us now consider the application of separative and conjunctive errors in establishing the main types of stemma.

If we have two witnesses, A and B, the stemma must be one of the three following types:

(II. 1a) A   (II. 1b) B   (II. 2) a (lost archetype)
$\mid$ $\mid$ $\diagup\,\diagdown$
B   A   A   B

If we find a separative error of A against B, then Type II. 1a is excluded. If we find a separative error of B against A, then Type II. 1b is excluded. If we find a separative error of A against B and one of B against A, then Types II. 1a and II. 1b are both excluded and Type II. 2 is proved.

If B is obviously later than A, of course no separative error of B is required to exclude Type II. 1b.

If we find a separative error of B against A, but none of A against B, the presumption in extensive texts is that we have Type II. 1a.

It is this inference which is the basis of the prevailing view that the oldest manuscript is the archetype of all the others in a great number of classical texts, e.g. the *Syntax* of Apollonius Dyscolus (*Wochenschr. für klass. Phil.* 1911, 25 ff.), those plays of Euripides which lack scholia (see above, § 27), Athenaeus 3–15 (*Byz. Zeitschr.* xxxv. 299 ff.). The *apparent* significant errors of the earlier tradition as against the later are the result of Byzantine conjectural criticism, which in its turn has had new light cast on it through the observation of these connexions.

In shorter texts there is also a slight probability that we have Type II. 2; this would mean that by chance no separative error against B had crept in during the period between a and A.

If we have three witnesses at our disposal, then we have twenty-two possible types of stemma. First of all we try to

discover, along the lines just indicated, whether one of the witnesses is the exemplar of one of the two others or of both. In
the latter case we have one of the two following types:

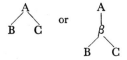

The decision depends on whether or not we can find a conjunctive error of B and C (β) against A.

If it can be shown that none of the three witnesses is the
exemplar of another, then 18 of the 22 types of stemma may be
excluded (6 in which one witness is the exemplar of one of the
two others, and 12 where one witness is the exemplar of both
the others); this leaves the following 4 possible types:

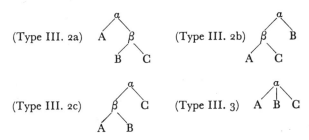

The decision depends on whether there is a conjunctive error in
two of these witnesses against the third (Types III. 2a–c), or
not (Type III. 3).

This conjunctive error must, however, at the same time be
also a separative error; for if it were of a kind capable of being
removed by conjecture we should not be able to exclude Type
III. 3.

Most conjunctive errors have no separative force, whereas most
separative errors can also be used as conjunctive errors. Many of the

so-called homoeoteleuta are separative errors which cannot be used as conjunctive errors, because on the one hand they are often so difficult to avoid that several copyists were almost bound to commit them independently, and on the other hand it was beyond the powers of medieval textual critics to remove them.

It is advisable to insert into the stemma references to the passages of the text ('indicative passages') where the indicative errors occur. If for instance we have Type III. 2a, we get the following scheme:

1 = separative error in C against B, to exclude $\begin{array}{c}C\\|\\B\end{array}$

2 = separative error in B against C, to exclude $\begin{array}{c}B\\|\\C\end{array}$

3 = separative error in A against β (B+C), to exclude $\begin{array}{c}A\\|\\\beta\\ \diagup\;\diagdown\\B\quad C\end{array}$

4 = conjunctive error, which is at the same time a separative error, in β (B+C) against A, to exclude $\begin{array}{c}\alpha\\ \diagup|\diagdown\\A\;B\;C\end{array}$

This type is preserved in its purity, e.g., in the Byzantine tradition of Herodotus as it appears since K. Hude introduced cod. Vat. 2369 (D) in his edition (O.C.T. 1926). I give the concordance of the above schematic stemma with Hude's sigla:

$$\alpha = L$$
$$A = \mathbf{a}\ (ABC)$$
$$\beta = \mathbf{d}\ (DRSV)$$
$$B = D$$
$$C = RSV$$

The only variant-carriers then are the manuscripts **a** and **d**, which are lost but can be reconstructed with certainty.

If we then have, in addition to these three witnesses, a fourth witness, D, its position in the stemma depends on whether D has one of these four indicative errors or not. If for instance D has the indicative error of A against β, we have only to establish the relation of D to A along the lines above indicated. If D has none of these four indicative errors, then we must investigate the relation of D to a. D may be (1) the exemplar of a, (2) a itself, (3) derived from a independently of A and β:

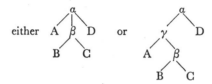

If D is obviously later than A, B, and C, then the first two of the three possibilities (1 and 2) are excluded. The decision between the last two depends on whether we find a conjunctive error which is at the same time separative in A+B against D or not.

[If we have four witnesses, the number of possible types of stemma amounts to 250, if we have five, to approximately 4,000, and so on in quasi-geometrical progression. 1949.]

The Romance scholar J. Bédier ('La tradition manuscrite du Lai de l'Ombre', *Romania*, liv (1928), 161 ff., 321 ff.) makes the, at first sight, startling remark that the three- (or more-) branched

type hardly ever occurs in stemmata in modern critical editions and that not only in the hyparchetypes, but in the archetype, so that the whole stemma is in two branches. Bédier does not adduce the Greek tradition but his remark applies here also.

But it is precisely in the three-branched type that the uses of stemmatics would be most clearly demonstrated; since in this case every 'peculiar reading' of one witness can be eliminated by the agreement of the remaining two, the critical apparatus in this type should not, in fact, show a single variant. But since we have no such apparatuses, the suspicion has been expressed that critics, in order to avoid being forced to renounce their free choice between the transmitted readings, have either lopped off the third branch (and any additional branches) or allowed two branches to fuse into one in defiance of the facts.

There is, however, a more innocent explanation of this. First of all we must remind ourselves that of the twenty-two types of stemma possible where three witnesses exist, only one has three branches (see above). Furthermore it is in the very nature of the medieval tradition that in the case of little-read texts three copies were rarely taken from the same archetype; more rarely still have all these copies, or descendants of each of them, survived; on the other hand where texts were much read there is a tendency for contamination to creep in, and where contamination exists the science of stemmatics in the strict sense breaks down. In the later sub-branches it would certainly have been easier to presuppose the existence, and survival, of three copies from the same archetype; but in these cases the editors were often able, without doing any harm, to avoid adducing more than two of these copies in order to reconstruct a hyparchetype of no stemmatic importance.

I may add here a word on the conception of 'families' (or 'classes') of manuscripts. There is no place for this conception in stemmatics strictly speaking; there are only individual witnesses such as the archetype and its separate descendants, and it is immaterial whether they survive or their existence is merely inferred. Where a tradition is uncontaminated we can never make the same assertion of a number of different witnesses:

either they derive from a common exemplar, in which case we may only speak of the exemplar, or one derives from another, in which case it must be eliminated. But where the stemmatic position still remains obscure the conception of 'families' may be helpful. We understand by it a group of witnesses shown by conjunctive errors to belong together as against other witnesses, but whose internal interrelations are of no importance for the moment and need not be discussed. We can then select the oldest member as representative of its family and eliminate without further ado any additional witnesses which are shown by a conjunctive error to belong to the family.

Finally let me call to mind the pleasing simile used by Otto Immisch to illustrate the conception of 'stemma', in his discussion of the 'formula for recension' (*Rezensionsformel*) (*Wie studiert man Philologie?* 2nd ed. (1920), 106). Just as the chemical formula settles the arrangement of the atoms in each molecule of a compound in unambiguous and unalterable fashion, so the stemma settles the relationship of witnesses for every passage in the text—*if* we have a virgin tradition. No specific has yet been discovered against contamination.

APPENDIX II

RETROSPECT 1956

THE success of this booklet with the bookseller has been considerably greater than any perceptible influence it has had on editions and studies in textual criticism which have appeared since 1927. The reasons for this may well be, firstly, that in the last thirty years no alternative introduction to this branch of scholarship has appeared and, secondly, that the abstract nature of the work has had a deterrent effect. There are no doubt also certain inadequacies in my treatment of the subject which I would gladly attempt to make good if they were brought to my attention whether privately or in public. Perhaps the following three excursuses may help to clarify some concepts peculiar to the subject which hitherto have been little discussed.

1. *Latent Evidence*

One of the more elementary tasks of 'stemmatics'—the demonstration of the dependence of one witness (B) on another (A), with the object of eliminating B as a witness—demands as a rule the previous demonstration of the absence of any 'separative error' in A as against B, i.e. the production of 'latent evidence'.

For the definition of 'separative error' see above, page 42. Errors in A which in their context could not be recognized as such at all, and consequently could provide no occasion for their elimination by conjecture, can be classified as 'separative errors' with more than usual assurance.

EXAMPLE. No copyist would notice the omission of line 14 of the *Bacchae* of Euripides in Laurentianus (L) as against the Palatinus (P).

COUNTER-EXAMPLE. In line 635 of the same play, the gap in L is so striking and its conjectural supplement by παρεῖται (so P) is so obvious (compare 683 παρειμέναι) that one can hardly class the error in L as a certain 'separative error'. It was precisely in the period between L and P that Byzantine conjectural criticism (Planudes, Triclinius) flourished.

Suppose the text of A to have been worked over by a relatively experienced scholar in the period between A and B, with the result that many obvious errors present in A are not to be found in B: in that case the 'latent evidence' would naturally only become apparent after a great deal of detailed work; all the 'better' readings of B must be produced and in each case the grounds on which they might be treated as conjectures must be explained. Consequently experience shows the advisability of placing the burden of proof in questions of dependence of this kind on whoever contests the dependence. He must at the very least demonstrate the existence of one certain 'separative error' in A as against B.

One certain instance is sufficient (as 100 doubtful instances would not be) to turn into potential variants all the peculiar readings of B as against A. The question how many of them must all the same be ranked as conjectures is of importance in the criticism of the text of Sophocles; see above, page 43 and *Gnomon*, xxv (1953), 441 f.

If the attempt to demonstrate the existence of the single 'separative error' fails and continues to fail, then the probabilities are in favour of the dependence of B upon A, that is of the editor's obligation to exclude B as a witness.

This applies to the cases enumerated above on page 44 and to countless similar cases. Recently G. R. Manton has added the demonstration that in several treatises of Plutarch the manuscript B derives from E (*C.Q.*xliii (1949), 97–100). With regard to Athenaeus, it has recently been pointed out that a scholium, of which the epitome of page 515 e of the text asserts that it stood in its exemplar, is to be found word for word in Marcianus (A), written in a hand which is later than A and earlier than Eustathius, our oldest witness for the epitome (*Byz. Z.* xlv (1952), 1f. with plate). Thus side by side with the 'latent evidence' we have a positive witness for the derivation of the epitome from A. That Eustathius was the author of the conjectures in the epitome can hardly be contested much longer.

2 'Recentiores, non deteriores'

With this chapter heading G. Pasquali has rightly emphasized (in chapter 4 of the book referred to on page vii above) that a witness which is later in date than another is not necessarily on that account also 'worse'. But the fact is that there are neither 'good' nor 'bad' witnesses, only dependent and independent ones, that is witnesses which are dependent on or independent of surviving manuscripts or manuscripts which can be reconstructed without their help. The age of a witness only comes into consideration in as far as the earlier cannot derive from the later. The oldest existing witness is always completely 'independent', whereas the independence of later witnesses, as against those which are earlier than themselves, must first be proved by 'separative errors'. Accordingly in the examination of witnesses with a view to their independence, the right course is to begin with the oldest but one and then to work through to the *recentiores* in chronological sequence; these recentiores will for the most part, though of course not always, turn out to be dependent. And at that point a halt must be called. 'All manuscripts should be collated and the results should be set out . . .; that might be even worse than idolizing one manuscript as the sole source of grace' (Wilamowitz, *Aristophanes* Lys. 1927, p. 62). 'Comburendi, non conferendi' (Cobet).

Modern English textual critics, in discussing problems of dependence in English printed books of the sixteenth and seventeenth centuries, have introduced the expression 'substantive' for the concept 'independent', thus expressing in positive terms that the peculiar readings of a witness may contain something of the 'substance' of a lost original which is missing from the remaining witnesses. The expression is considerably clearer than 'independent', but I hesitate to adopt it.

3. Diagnostic conjectures

In general we distinguish only between 'right' and 'wrong' conjectures and are inclined to reject out of hand any that are not 'right'.

However, according to the views expressed above in §§ 13 ff., the conjecture, whether 'right' or 'wrong', is an important part of the *examinatio*, that is, the investigation whether the transmitted text is or is not the best conceivable. To determine the value of conjecture as a means of investigation it is unimportant whether conjectures made for this purpose, that is 'diagnostic' conjectures, succeed in carrying conviction in detail, or whether they merely represent, as against the tradition, the 'lesser evil', or whether they are completely wide of the mark. It is a matter for the nicety of the editor's discrimination to decide which of such conjectures deserve mention in the *apparatus criticus*. Before he rejects a conjecture without reason given, he should ask himself whether he would feel himself able, should the conjecture be the transmitted text, to recognize this as corrupt. In cases of doubt he should, more often than is done today, place a crux in the text or a '*locus suspectus*' in the *apparatus criticus*, to protect himself against the surprises which a newly discovered witness or a cogent emendation can have in store for the all too trusting defender of the tradition.

To the examples given above in Chapter E, a particularly instructive example may be added here: Ovid, *Fast.* 3. 725 f. (vulg.)

> carminis huius opus causas exponere, quare
> vilis anus populos ad sua liba vocet.

Although *vilis anus* makes no sense and although both *sua* and the context demand that Bacchus appear as the subject, the vulgate

remained uncontested until, in 1929, the reading *vitisator* came
to light as a well-supported variant. It clearly preserves what the
poet wrote (*Vitisator* cited by Macrobius, *Sat.* 6. 5. 11, from
Vergil and Accius) and would have been found by conjecture in
the course of a systematic *examinatio*. The malignant corruption
presumably arose through the miswriting of *vitis* as *vilis*, which
was then made worse by the conjecture of *anus* based on line
765. For similar problems in the text of Horace's lyric poems
compare *Studi italiani di filologia classica*, 1956 (Memorial volume
for G. Pasquali).

BIBLIOGRAPHY

1. Theoretical treatments and collections of examples:

A. Boeckh, *Enzyklopädie und Methodologie der philologischen Wissenschaften*, 1877, 179–209 (a posthumous publication).

F. Blass, article 'Kritik' in I. von Müller's *Handbuch der klassischen Altertumswissenschaft*, I, 2nd edn., 1892, 249–89.

R. C. Jebb in *A Companion to Greek Studies*, ed. L. Whibley, 1906, 610–23.

J. P. Postgate in *A Companion to Latin Studies*, ed. J. E. Sandys, 1910, 791–805.

L. Havet, *Manuel de critique verbale appliquée aux textes latins*, 1911, 481 pp., quarto: an important book, but the useful theoretical sections are lost in the mass of examples, not all of which are important or appropriate.

F. W. Hall, *Companion to Classical Texts*, 1913, 108–98: this section of the book has many well-chosen examples and valuable suggestions. (The reader is warned that the rest of the book, except the useful section on the nomenclature of manuscripts, is no longer up to date.)

G. Pasquali: *see* Preface.

2. Papyri: E. Lobel's publications of Sappho, Alcaeus, Callimachus, &c. in the successive volumes of the Oxyrhynchus Papyri that have appeared since 1925.

3. Layout of a critical edition: O. Stählin, *Editionstechnik*, 2nd edn., 1914, contains many practical hints worth noting; cf. A. Delatte and A. Severyns, *Emploi des signes critiques*, 1938, on which see U. Knoche, *Göttingischer Gelehrter Anzeiger*, ccii, 1940, 515–31.

4. Critical editions and studies of the history of individual texts:

Wilamowitz's *Herakles*, vol. i, 1889 (last reprinted in 1921 with the title *Einleitung in die griechische Tragödie*) is still of fundamental importance. See also Wilamowitz's other editions of texts and writings on textual history. Among other modern editions of texts see in particular O. Schroeder's *Pindar* (ed. mai. 1900); A. E. Housman's *Lucan* (1926) and *Manilius* (ed. mai. 1903–30); R. Pfeiffer's *Callimachus* (vol. i, 1949; vol. ii, 1953).

INDEX

PRINTED IN GREAT BRITAIN
AT THE UNIVERSITY PRESS, OXFORD
BY VIVIAN RIDLER
PRINTER TO THE UNIVERSITY